who shot the rose

NOURISH CRUZ

First paperback edition: May 2021.

Book design by Studio Creative Group.
Layout by Angela Mark.
Edited by Timothy Lindner and John Lunar Richey.
Published by Nourish Narratives.

ISBN: 978-0-578-88044-0
LCCN: 2021907424

Dedication

I dedicate this book to my high school poetry teacher, Ms. Perez who taught me how to savor moments, as if a pen dragging across a page could slow down time.

To Big Mike, my Youth Slam Poetry Coach, now Co-Host of "What's the Word on Cherry Street", who never let me doubt my abilities as an artist, who showed me how internally rewarding it is to give art and love back to the community.

To my nieces and nephews, who will hopefully grow to breathe fresher air and live in a more peaceful place than the one that exists today. Like Greta Thunberg, may they become brave little voices that inspire the masses.

Table of Contents

Fix The Static

Interrupt the broadcast.
Global warming on the forecast
soldiers dying in the bomb blast
mothers crying on my Comcast.

Fix the static!

Gun control on demand
assault rifles on the band
got Teachers on the stand.
Come on, Preacher, what's your plan?

Fix the static!

Netflix and chill
till Epstein tried to grab it.
Netflix and chil-dren
are being trafficked.
Netflix and chill
entertained by havoc.

Fix the static!

"It's 10pm do you know where your children are?"

Plugged into "World Star"
the world's far
till it's your son shot 41 times in HD
till it's your pocket feeling the poverty
till it's your womb as legislative property.

Fix the static!

Equal Rights on demand

2 Women, wedding bands.
How many deaths?
Save the Trans. "Love is Love"
understand?

Interrupt the broadcast.
Made Muslims outcasts?
The threat wears a white mask.
Have to watch who you walk past.

"Grab them by the pussy."

Fix the static!

Who Shot the Rose?

One more dreamer
flower girl
peddling promise, pistoled.

One less rose scented sidewalk to
shepherd the senseless
into sanctuary.

Hit by a stray bullet.
She tried to write away bullets.
NRA, oh they portray bullets.

Award-winning writer
a rose called Parks
a little Rosa Parks
front seat furious for freedom.
Dodging delinquent gunfire, daily.

Sadly seeds of the street
stem like statues
end as tombstones.

Withering in her mother's arms
she was only 13.
We all held the gun.
We didn't do enough.
Some of us did nothing.

One more dreamer
flower girl
planted painfully
watered by tears
gardened in eternal light.

In memory of Sandra Parks.

3

Final Exam

Remember those high school kids
dressed in black
becoming night knights
in the daylight
to fight the world
that looked away
like they were glares.

Remember those high school kids
"Columbining" their school
bet they looked right at the shooters
like they were fucking scared
for that final exam unprepared.

Like those shortys
wearing short skirts and booty shorts
taking shortcuts for cash
out of class
to shake their ass
to be with small-minded men
who in the long run
ended their lives by cutting them.

And those who wore red, long sleeves
like Valentines
dripping from their wrists
because no one wanted to talk to them
hold their hand long enough
for the loneliness to stop.

The violence never stops.
They couldn't end the abuse
or hunger at home
so they fed off anger
took it out on kids
who couldn't defend themselves.

Carrying knives in their lunch box
AKs in their backpacks.
Inhaling chalk and gunpowder
as shots ring louder.

Bullies picking away
at more than childhood acne.

A nine-year-old killed himself
not because he was gay
because no one taught the other kids
how to appreciate the beauty in, different.

We lost our principles.
We failed our students.

Write this 10 times on the board:

I will not bring a gun to school.
I will not bring a gun to school.
I will not!

When I was a kid
I thought meeting on the playground
after school was dangerous.
Till I was taught a freshly sharpened #2 pencil
and a creative mind could be dangerous!

One day
I will make a difference
when I "write it into existence."

"Dear Congress,

I was afraid to go back to school today.
I can't focus.
Isaiah's chair is empty
and his mother's eyes are filled with tears."

There's blood splatter that they missed
on the desk leg, a pencil that rolled
under the closet door after the first shot
an alarm they thought was a drill
that won't stop
ringing in traumatized children's ears.

When was the last time
you all sat at the kitchen table
motivated your child until they were able
held your son or daughter
until they were stable?

One day
I'll take a gun out of a child's mind
put a pen in their hand
so they can massacre
their negative feelings on paper
before one more mother
has to bury her baby.

Queen Moves

There are Queens among us
who pluck gems from their crowns
lay jewels to replace the stones
that have crumbled.

There are Martin Kings among us
who decree no man nor bravest Knight
dare slay a daughter's dreams

and there are Jesters
who play fiddles
while dragons burn villages
who tap the cobblestone
to mask the shepherd's cry.

Let us pray to the Bishop
come sunrise, even our pawns have power.

Today Kamala Harris
tomorrow our daughters reign.

Blue Soldier

My thoughts, they suffer
from the world's disregard for integrity
lack of respect.
Trying to reflect whatever goodness is left

while I dwell upon the endangered futures
of little ones carrying big guns
living on the run.

Many are cast in shadows of alleyways
seldom happy days
staying true to a color
not to themselves
becoming gang members
even at the age of 12.

A sight to see
not the one to be.
Smoking up his lungs
even killing his own loved ones.

Such a tragedy.
Helping all I could
still had him mad at me.
Didn't have that bad in me.

He was a thug with a gun
without a wife, with a son
about to be a lonely one.

Preaching about respect and pride
when all I saw was harm.
He was taking a new meaning
to the right to bear arms.

Having pride in being a blue soldier
little did he know
his life would soon be over.

He was all suited up
dressed in blue
this time laying on the ground
with blood flowing through.

He had a passion for being a thug.
Took a slashing because he was
wearing a different color from another
walking down the street.
Sad because in many places
it happens every other week.

Told him to aim for the stars
but he couldn't reach.
Missed church every Sunday
so he couldn't hear the preacher teach goodness.
All the knew was "hoodness."
Wished that he could have bliss.

It's too late
the precious life he missed out on.
My heart pours out
but more weapons are still drawn.

Morality couldn't set him free
if only someone would've told him
this wasn't his destiny.

Melting I.C.E.

We are the children of many tongues
somehow homeless in harmony
crying in cages
for our tears to root us into American soil.

We will not become homegrown terrorist
in your oppression.

See us stem higher than fucking Trump's wall!

When you tell them to speak English
it's like telling them to curse their Mother.

Sold her wedding ring
so you could keep your father's last name
bought a ticket to Ellis Island
screamed, "**FREEDOM!**"
like she came
in that accent
from that country you shame.

See, America can get fucked by Columbus
but its bastard children
will be nothing like the few tarnished of Spain
will not be romanced by a battalion
and the silk they stole.

We are not all plagued or pirates.
We came here to persevere.

I am the 6 digit tattoo
on your Jewish grandfather's forearm

the smallpox vaccination scar
on your Dominican mother's left shoulder

the laceration on your first generation
Mexican help that you pay penny wages to.

I am watered down by tears
and my grandmother's bleached skin.
Hiding from lynchmen
hesitating at whites only fountains.

I am the ape & the wetback.
You are the "Make America Great Again"
cutting off blood supply to the brain, cap.

We are bred
to be architects, farmers, champions.

We will never be stripped
of our DNA in this USA.

We are "America the Beautiful"
in our home away from home.

Thrive
OR Thirst?

**You will never be a starving artist
if you feed the people inspiration.**

Beautiful Woman

There are too many women brushing
bitterness out of their hair in despair
touching up teardrops on their
foundation the cracks are too deep.
Oh, how she weeps.

It's no wonder why
women take so long in the restroom.
Perk your breasts
fix your mess room.

Twenty pounds too large
Twenty pounds too light
until they are hollow
all for a 🖤 or a 👍Follow .

Telling people that her scars
are birthmarks when there are bruises
buried behind the blush.

Glossy layer of insecurity
lips like a red flag
subtle sadness in her swag.
Carrying too much unnecessary shit
in her bag.

Drinks till she stag.
Girl, lift your chin up!

Add an inch to her heels
for every time that she feels
put below her worth

Depression births
under her skirt.

Waiting for a flirt to ease the hurt.
All it does is hinder healing.
Has empty sex to numb her feelings.

Shit, he's flexing and she's feeling.
To the wrong one she's kneeling.
She's so revealing.

Lace-back
False-lashed
wing-eyed yet crashing.

Botox smiles barrier her trials.
Honey, it's okay to cry.

You used to love yourself
in a messy bun
pushing pennies in Payless.

You had too much power
in principle to pretend
you were a pervert's "Pretty."

In your pimpled face, crooked smile
happy was your style.
Your confidence made you cute.
Your worth, they can't compute.

You are priceless!

Pride

This is for the boy who tried on his Mother's makeup
felt beautiful for the first time.

For the fathers that love their sons
but held their trans daughters tighter
knowing intolerance still exists.

For the girl who joined the football team
once told her hair wasn't long enough
clothes not tight enough
not fitting in but finding her true self.

This is for everyone who loves someone
for their soul, not their gender.

For the great people that we lost and still remember
for the Matthew Shepards, Marsha Johnsons
49 who never made it home from the Pulse nightclub.

For the two lesbians on the London bus
who were beaten
and the beauty between them
that could not be bruised.

For all the times I was told, I was just confused.

This is for every he, she or they pronoun
who crosses the street holding their partners hand
knowing there is a community
that respects their love
for being progressive and rising above.

For anyone afraid to come out
I pray you find your freedom within:

This is where bravery begins.

Don't You?

Don't you love
to see them rise
defy gravity with their joyous skip
make their mommas proud
inspire someone
they never knew was watching?

Don't you love
when they pass mirrors
knowing their inner beauty is reflecting
self-respecting?

Don't you love
to traject the pain
seeing them reign
where the ground once stopped
their sinking, negative thinking
so your heart had time to heal their heels
so they could chase their goals?

Don't you love
when they have nothing but a tear
a desperate ear
to speak the answer
to rid their cancer?

Don't you love without motive
to be a motivation?

Don't you love?

Viva Puerto Rico

I'm the history of the word
Taino Indian verb.
Sending smoke signals and courier birds.

My slang carried Caribbeans
to the free land
between lines and verses.

Learned how to read and write
by writing life back into our leaders in hearses.
Columbus brought Measles and curses.

Tried to take our cotton and gold
how the story is told
but we are too proud to be silent.

Viva Puerto Rico!

Many say we're a lazy tongue
but they complicated the songs we sung.
Because "laaaa" is a song
"the" can't sing.
Derived from Arawak
survived in Latin swing.

My people bring
culture to land and sky.
Broke bread and beat drums
to Zemi Gods till we amplified.

Survived genocide!

Played poems off maracas
dressed in sea shells
while medicine men spoke spells.

Even coquis sing our songs
while we sleep.
Wake to crows and canter
parrandas y pasteles.

Palates pineapple and passion fruit
perfumed Pueblos with Panaderias.

Tasting the same plantains off plantations
our great grandmothers gardened
how intoxicating!

Drunk off sugar cane turned rum.
Mountains echoing our native tongue.
Flags in the breeze that we've hung.

Captivated
diving into cascades of crystal waters
that leave eyes thirsty
and mouths memorializing
La Isla del Encanto.

Epiphany

I am here today
because I am tired of living in fear.

I know now
why they were scared to give their names
why they tucked in their David stars and crosses
sacrificed to prevent losses
turned their family tree into plywood.

How many people
had to board up their homes
their stores
give up everything
swallow their diamond rings.
Suffocating in sorrow
before they even reached the gas chamber.

"JUDE JUDEN!"
I heard that Nazi knocked on a Jewish door.
Their hearts beat so loud in their minds
they thought the SS could hear them.
It was the faucet running.
They stood there, helpless.
Saw what happens when people start running.

BANG!

We remember, Anne Frank.

I heard of the threatening phone call
Malcolm X's wife got from the KKK.
Her tears drowned out the sound
than the house was lit on fire.
She couldn't cry enough to extinguish the flames.

And there was George Floyd...
Will his ancestors ever breathe?

The Ignorant:

"The culprits…
I can't tell you what they looked like
what exactly they were wearing.
I know it was them
eating that smelly food they eat
talking gibberish amongst themselves.
I keep telling them to speak English.

Taking over our good neighborhoods
stealing our jobs for cheap.

And them girly boys
that Marsha Johnson in his sister's makeup bag.
I'll beat that sodomite
till he knows good and well how to procreate.

Yea…it was a long time ago.
I can't tell us apart so much now
Oswald killing our president.
Looked like my friend's white son
shooting up that school.

Can't even blame it on them, colored boys.
We're all messed up!"

I'm Free!

What are bars but silver jewels
an accent to the face of hope
encasing black diamonds trying to cope.
Not guilty.

I am free in a verse.
I'm not cursed.
Carried away by the wind
on a wrinkled verdict page.

I stopped counting the days.
May my past not become my penitentiary.

I am present
not in a park
not in the dark
not me!

Glittered by a tear.
I'm no prisoner here.
I've been free
to dance when the lights are out
and positive words are whispers.

In a borrowed bed springs in my back.
I still find a way to smile in my sleep.

Wake, to the sun reaching out the window
reminding me a warmth within' exist.

What are 4 walls but a box.
I am a gift!
Not guilty.

For Trisha Meili and The Central Park Five

Transgressions

Rushing every day to leave to work
to get home
to ignore the people around us
while checking our IGs and Facebook for memes.

We critique ourselves on Snapchat
scrolling filters when we could be
working on building health, muscle and confidence.

On our last day
if we are fortunate enough to say goodbye
all we want to do is take our time
with people we love
not our selfie
to see tomorrow.

Yet every day before
we didn't want to get up.
We wanted to keep sleeping.
We dwelled on anger and sadness
instead of laughing it off
embracing positivity, having appreciation.

We hated on politicians and watched violent videos
when we could have been teaching our family humanity
educating ourselves on religion and culture
not just our own.

I am not innocent of these transgressions
but I tell you, I've heard too many stories
of unseen tomorrows to not try my best to smile
on cloudy day.

Contrast

Just because bruises are harder to see
on brown skin
it doesn't make them any less painful.
Why does it take the contrast
of blood on concrete
for people to notice a problem?

Shouting!

Did you hear the church bell break
the bomb that shook Syria
the boy crying under the rubble?

Have you heard the caravan of footsteps
the bodies falling
the gas hissing?

Did you hear the screams
of virgin Indian girls
the chains of concentration camps
in Cuba, China.

the refrigerator reverberation
in vacant Venezuela
the trash being rummaged for food
the bellies rumbling?

Did you hear the jail cell slam shut
the racist cop's eyes open
when the system showed it's broken
truth finally spoken?

Did you hear the soldier's flag drop
the sound of his metal leg
dragging against the pavement
the gasp when the federal government missed
their payment?

Did you hear the newspaper turning
politicians laughing
the money being counted
the silenced
the speechless
the sin?

Rainy Day in Newark

Through the sickness and the slaughter
still are your sons and daughters.
Sipping survival like Flint water
Newark urban experiment water.

Consume enough to get by
but we die a little
enough to get high
so we fly a little.
We can't get far enough
from the famine.
Hard to think much less examine.

When you tip the well
wish them well first.
This goes beyond thirst
progress reversed.

I've seen tears concealed by rain
metal bars on window panes
children playin'
with paper boats made out of old food stamps
eviction letters.
Notes with "Toxic Lead" headers
gentrification adult bed wetter
blow through urban gutters
by Tenant sighs
and Landlord lies.

Here cancer walks with shiny shoes
and a lifted chin.
Tap water pours the same color
as Latin skin.
Dying like we're on the Titanic
because of the class we're in.

Soaked in sweat and sin.
Borders death and grim.

Beautiful brown stones turning white
forget being polite
you can't white power wash poverty!
Saw them waterhose people.
Waiting for the SoHo sequel

Race not recession
praying for a blessin'.
Extermination
not really a united nation

Lady Liberty's legs are spread.
Chaos is crowning
we are 40 days and nights past drowning.

The levee broke
are we really woke?
For days Louisianan watched the bodies float.
We are brainwashed, sinking
immersed in negative thinking.

What was our president drinking?
Tossing napkin rolls
while death tolls were rising
called it enterprising, not surprising!

We're thirsty!
This is unearthly
to allow so much preventable death.
Ain't got much left.
Puerto Rico put 3 thousand to rest.
Worried about a vape
when the Amazon
is putting smoke our chests.
Government's priorities a mess.

Where's the water for the fire?
Survival only for the highest buyer.

My glass is half empty
filled with political piss.
Would you drink this?

Praying
Petals

And all her thorns fell
back into the Earth
to pierce an unworthy ground
while she became a rose
on Mother Mary's Crown.

Protest or March?

Fallen soldiers
I wonder if their sons and daughters would ever march
salute a nation that some say has failed them.
Vulnerable to an inner battle
when the borders of their Forefather's arms
tragically seized to protect them
a landmine, a suicide bomber, a bullet, PTSD.

I wonder if they'd sit proudly reaching
for a triangular folded flag
while gazing at a purple heart
saying goodbye to an empty casket
holding dog tags
squeezing the shit out of their mother's hands
to keep her from falling apart.

Too many fighting a war with tears
breathing in the smell of fresh turned soil
risen six feet in defeat.

He was so proud to wear that uniform
but now he cowers in the shower
trying to wash memories only he can see on his skin.
Did we really win?

I wonder if they'd be the first to make it back home
never mentally leave the war they thought they left.
I wonder if they'd go back to avenge their father's death?

Would they ever protest or march?
Into the deafening sounds
"Infidel!" bullet ricochet and screams
"Pigs, Murderers," bats hitting SWAT shields and marines.

Homegrown terrorists
wiring pipe bombs
tearing at smoke bombs
rioting in the streets
with no one sane to lead em'
would they fight for freedom?

The Messenger

Feed me.
Breathe me like the air
that once filled your lungs.
Made from the dust:
the next chosen one.

I've got the help of the deceased
death's adversaries
living vicariously
incorporating words into my vocabulary
in positions so creative they're beyond
imaginary.

Hints in dreams
I wake up
try to figure out what they mean.
Sometimes, I can only remember
the crease on the page.
I spend all day
till I remember what they were trying to say.

I went fishing and caught the Lord.
All faiths absorbed.
Didn't really know who I was
until I explored the risen seas
of what there is to believe
from Qur'an, Islam
to Buddhist, enlightenment
Atheism, wherever belief went.

God sent.
This is my copyrighted content.
Please don't ask me
where the disciple con went.
This is no convent.

Jesus Fire

All I hear are…
SHOTS FIRED!!!
The burning heart of Jesus is the only shooting fire.
Sinners retire
apostles admire
and we become one with the Sire.

Heavenly empires
each Sunday with flooded doors
praying for children we resurrect from blooded floors.

Hail Mary as mothers of God
you can't ignore
our peace is poor.
We litter our streets with war!

Full of Grace.
I'm far beyond this place.
We should be done with race.
I'm alien.

I practice mental migration.
With Obama
I thought we joined forces
had a black and white inauguration
With Trump we lost integration.

Why are the sons still bearing the sins of their fathers
innocent immigrant children being caged like robbers?

By door knocking Jehovah's Witness raptures
most bothered.
Preaching, "The Lord is with Thee"
but no one reads the pamphlets.
Sorry Luke John and Paul weren't Hamlet.

Sorry immaculate conception
didn't turn you, "Fifty Shades of Grey."
I pray
till I'm intimate
with the Holy Spirit.

I hear it.
Names in vain
only calling **GOD** only when in pain.
So many slain.
I'm so drained.
I'm like the falling towers.

"9/11 Never forget"
It's past October now.
You don't even have to be black
to get pulled over now.
They've got turbans and saris
on the shoulder now.

It's time to arm myself.
I'm bullet shell filled with mustard seed
firing faith.

I'm peace pipe
higher than Heaven on Earth
and a pound of Kush.

I'm Jesus Fire
and burning bush!

Nostalgia

Past race
I race past color to feel presence
where darkness isn't black
and canvas isn't white
when a soul is simply pure light.

I look to conscience to define a being.

Past senses
when we all look the same before we had eyes
when we were closer than hugs
before we had arms
when we knew no physical harm
only inner beauty.

What was beautiful then
was that we knew everything
before our bodies
put foul odors into our noses
profanity into our ears
tears into our eyes
the taste of things our tongues
should've never tasted in the first place.

Before hearts hated or minds lust
before eyes saw or hands touched
places, things, people
that they shouldn't have
when we were souls
before religion
before racism
before war
when Satan was faithful to God
when we were all faithful to each other.

before an angel fell
before Abel took his last breath
before death.

Subway Symphony

I caught his illness in the carbon
because all the trees were
rolled and smoked.

I caught his famine in the Big Apple, Madison
Garden because Adam and Eve sinned and choked.

I caught the shivers in the cold shoulders
he got from the rich.
As if it wasn't bad enough
his blanket was minimized to a stitch.

I caught some rain
that slid off his tongue, from his lips
put it into the Empire State
of his cataract eyes.
So he could look up into the sky scrapers
see the CNN billboard
of Hurricane Katrina's…Hurricane Maria's
sad puddle.

I caught some change
flipped it into the wishing well
of his palm.
I wished him well with a psalm
said, "God bless you"
and there was no rebuttal.

He was a resident of the underground studio caves
where ears show they love sound waves
produced & played
reduced or paid if impressed.

I caught a smile when he heard
"Please" and "Thank you"
after my favorite subway jam request.

There was embedded passion in his wrinkled fingers.
Saw the history of an assassin
in his knuckles and wrinkled fingers.

The subway passing
but the echo of (mic static)
"Please stay clear of the closing doors"
and urine smell still lingers.

Poverty a melody, a symphony

I caught his heartbeat
in the rush hour traffic footsteps
on Yankee chewing gum
New York Times, littered pavement.

I caught the angry, sacred
heavy breathing imprisoned.
Do your Time Square
in a cardboard box enslavement.

As blood leaks like his piss down broken cracks
from the enemies of those who pack
their guardian angel in their slacks.

Uptown to Downtown
Crosses on stolen chains
Bloodied t-shirts triggering past crimes in the brain.

Tapping on trash cans
while you're jamming to your iPod on the train.
Struggling to make some change.

He said he's been trying to change
But even if he changed into suit and tie
he couldn't put an address on a resume
a pay phone number
for them to call today.

poverty a melody, a symphony
change in plastic cups
and handcuffs.
"Spare me some change?"
or "Give me all your money!"
sounds like music.

I caught him!
Playing soul music
the last possible notes off broken strings
and rusty horns
to personify the beauty that could still
come out if his deteriorating body.

Playing blues.
Singing the pink back onto his cheeks
the purple off his lips
the red out his eyes
till his last verse turned people green with envy
made them forget for 2 beats
that he was just a poor man.

While he captured them...
I caught him
beat up some dude that stole his only quarter
that looked at him like he was less than a human
that spit on his cardboard house
that thought he would use the money
on drugs instead of food.

I caught him
beat music onto faces in perfect melody
like notepaper
sculpt every victim's profile into the Republican
that had no rhythm in his chest with his fist
yell, **"I EXIST!"**
sit right back down
and play his music.

Previously published in "Big Hammer, Volume 20"

Revival

Sometimes you need to run out of breath
to fill yourself
with something far more vital
than oxygen.

The Unexpected

You don't know joy
until you listen for God
to answer your desperate prayers
and hear your inner child laugh instead.

Happy Birthday!

We are born
crying into this world
as if we could hear chaos
from our mother's womb.

Happy Birthday!

To the babies who were aborted
before they got to see a Birthday.

To the 13-year-old Jewish boys
who become men.
How much could they know then?

To the 18-year-olds
who give birth to new hormones at the strip club.

To the 21-year-olds
who reverse baptize themselves in alcohol.

To the 100-year-old seniors
who become **IMMORTAL** in their Dementia.

The reborn Christians
forced to give up their gay lovers
to find Christ yet find strife.

A toast, to the day we fall in love and beat hatred
to the day we cheat death and beat cancer.

To the day we wish on candles
for something far greater than ourselves.

We are born!

Resurrection of Rhythm

Dancers, Resurrect!
Righteous feet Plie'
pointed like pyramids
wake Pharaohs from their tombs
to cross our Nile.

Hips shift like tectonic plates
under the ocean
sail Titanic like dreams
back to the surface.
Poets Erupt volcanic cheer
spitting liquid fire into the crowd.
Voices too powerful to be
extinguished.

Musicians,
"Mic check 1- 2."
Make them tremble
at the sound of your thunder.
Strike drums like lightning.

Can you hear me?
It's time to **AMPLIFY** your-self!

Resurrect!

Iridescent in their sweat and passion
like pearls emerging from the coral
like diamonds forming
under the pressure.

Heat, set a fire with their soles.
Dancing with their souls.

Fluid arms melting icebergs
like pterodactyls out of the Ice Age
to spread their wings arabesque
break the ceiling
show the world
there can be blue sky again!

Metal tap shoes like ice picks
into cold hearts, works of art.

Dancing diamonds
playing prodigies
preaching poetry
in every corner of the stage
filling voids
healing struggles.

Resurrect from the rubble.

Resurrect!

Dream

If you thought only Jesus could walk on water
you must have forgotten how to get to the moon
on a cardboard rocket ship.
Our faith is limitless.

Lord Laced

I hide my soul in my soles
so when my world is turned upside down
you know what God knows
not just my dirt.

Void

If you truly understood my darkness
I'd be the sun with its eyes closed.

I'd be the star you've been admiring
that died light years ago.

I'd be a pearl off Heaven's gate
fallen into a black hole.

I was so dark
hypoxic blue
a white nothing.

Than my eardrums burst
like a thousand last breaths
blowing me back into light
as I was ready to give up the fight.

Was a vampire's reflection
on a bloodied blade.

By grace I was saved.

Keep Pushing

There is no greater win
than the confidence
that made you believe you would
than the dignity
to give a congratulations
when you don't.

Construt

I knew not how to love
till I learned how to show desire
with my hands in my pockets
and my eyes closed.

How to give without thinking
about how much I'd have left
yet keep self respect.

How to smile
when the world around me isn't
to unleash an indisputable joy
to achieve a requited love.

Love

There are some scars
I wish to publish
before my body writes a romance novel
about my soft skin and where I've been.
I've healed since Chapter 2.

Find Me A Woman

Find me a woman
that keeps her tongue sacred
shows her heart naked.
Touches herself with ambition
requires respect for admission.

Show me a woman
that hides a beautiful secret
for someone who'd keep it
for someone who'd seek it.

Find me a woman
unafraid to get deep
that will be a dream, awake and in sleep.

Show me a woman
that is faithful
who is grateful
that is graceful.

Show me a woman
that loves- herself.

She Deserves

The one that called the weed a flower
the children Kings, Queens and future President
the homeless sir and ma'am.
She was the one
to bestow bounty on a good day
smile during tribulations
to embrace life lessons.

She was the one
holding the door
who wrote the letter instead of the text
who'd pray for what ever you desired
if you lost faith.

She was the one
listening to the world
like every footstep was song
like every stranger's heart could heal
with a "hello."

Could she teach me how to love
the way she greets the day
the way she thanks the night?

Could she teach me how to love
with her kind of effort
her joy in giving
her beauty of the moment
so I can love her, just the same.
She deserves.

Mind Vs. Heart

On the frontline of temptation
I waited for you.
Dressed as a soldier of love
heart on my sleeve.

Might be hard to believe
wishing your last name was attached to my chest
a medal of honor on my ring finger.

My smile waving proudly in the war winds
while Cupid arrows burst in mid air
flying within' the strands of your hair.

Saved movements and revolutions
for your cause
my body more faithful to you
than any other woman's nation be-cause
you are something worth fighting for!

Lips
FORWARD MARCH!
Loading cannons to puncture emotion
through the battle wounds
others left on your heart.

Cocking the rifle of my arms to hold your fire.
Looking down your barreled eyes
knowing this might be my only shot.

Slow Down

A scratch of skin
a breath as I pull her hair
the split of a bitten lip.

Slow down.

The fall of a pillow
the crackle of a candle
a gentle turn of the bed sheet.

I held her
until the weight of her burden blew
as free as my breath through her hair.

Listening for sentiment in our stillness
between moans
her ear upon my chest
my lips on her forehead.

Can you feel me?
between your fingers
falling only deeper
into the crease of your smile
when all the rest of you is exposed.

In a space they couldn't adore with lust
In a position, they couldn't partake without trust.

Can I wake to you
if I take it slow?

Polaris

Joining oceans with lands
so the 4 corners of the Earth
met on the palms of our hands

so Heaven was on the equator
of our hearts
so we'd always know where to go back
and start.

Never apart.

Cosmic Copulation

Orion's belt fell
yet gravity cannot divert
the way she orbits my shoulders.

We connect
erogenous zones
like constellations
cosmic copulation.

Zodiacs align
ecliptic kisses.
Nostalgic novas
like granted shooting stars
fading into candlelight.

Kinetic noons
magnetic moons
There is no space between us.

Linen on Lips

Undressing her
folding the innocence
away from her shoulders
pressing her fibers like silk covered spine.
I slide my arms into her bareness
like sleeves.

Line my lips
on the linen trimmed back of her neck.
Quilt warm along her thighs.
Fit right into her size.

A stitch we thread
where knees grow weak.
Once silent skin
now moans to speak.

Closer

Our eyes had a conversation
while our lips stared at each other.

Breathing each other
like we were each other's last breath.
Trying to catch our breath.

Whispering words
that caressed our cheeks
before they touched our ears.

I wanted to kiss your heart
before I kissed your lips
so I went further
kissed your forehead
before I kissed your neck.

Was that close enough?

Dandelion
Wishes

Tears are not meant to water thorns.
Blood does not bloom like red roses.

Battle of Broken

We've lost good women
to The Battle of Broken.
dropped their shields
gripped their heels
got tired of hopin'.

Lost too many women
Seen him toss too many women.

Till death do they part
fist bleed from broken mirrors
like her shattered heart.

She grieves till it gets clearer
than it's back at start.

Friends told her to leave him
but she couldn't break her vows
with his ring around her neck
where do we draw the line
between commitment and self-respect?
What type of image is he trying to project?

He gives her flowers
to say he's sorry
when she's half buried
in the bathroom floor
their is only so much shit a woman can endure.
No more!

Her daughter paints pictures
of her in black and blue
told her teachers that home
was the fucking zoo.

I've brought some women back to life
when they thought their only option
was a kitchen knife
when they thought they wouldn't make it
through the night.

You don't know what love is
what having to step over a trail of blood is
what having to pull her body in depression
out of the tub is.

It's not enough to call her beautiful
when she's been beaten and branded
when he's cheating, she's stranded.

I've spent so much time
mending malice
sucking poisons out of women's lips
so they could speak of their passions again
so they can be strong
if they ever pass him again.

Nearly lost good a woman to The Battle of Broken
stepped in made her feel like a token
complimented depths that were never once spoken.

Lost too many women
Lost too many women

Had to cross so many women
give them new provisions
free them from their prison.

Sweet Dreams

I know too much about self-preservation
to not love away bitterness

to not give weight to my words
after hearing empty promises

to give a blessing
succeeding affliction.

I sleep soundly this way.
My conscience tucks me in.

Ignited

To touch is pain
holding onto a flame
my hands are seared
with her impression.

These scars unseen
what burnt in between
unknowing what my heart
has yet to extinguish.

There once was a flame.
Now there's just a candle
in the window.

She Speaks

Cavemen slid their sticks
like I was dirt and sand.

Lie painted by his hand.
Wrote messages in cuneiform
but I was never uniform.

His rules I'd break
like 10 commandments
when she read my skin like braille
when she held me like the grail.

The stars have told our story before
Mayans ever spoke.

Sent signal to the heavens
in cloud of pink and smoke.

She was my sun god in hieroglyphics
pen prolific that'd never dry.

I read it somewhere on a scroll that
true love never dies.

She speaks my language.

Crucifixion

I am Eve's daughter
clutching Eden's clover
snakes whispering on my shoulder.

Praying that somewhere after atonement
there is a garden of paradise
another land of milk and honey
another miracle where water turns to wine.
I have faith in the divine.

I will be the last cursed womb
birth blessings like baptisms
cleansed crimson
ready to "tell it on the mountain"
plant my flag like I reached Everest.
I am above their prejudice.

He was the king of the Jews
and I was the Queen of …
Dodging brimstone
because they couldn't see the God in me
like I'm Judas's progeny.

Walking down the crooked path
into the hell, Christians said I would go
carrying my rainbow.
while the public threw "Fag, Dyke and Fruit" at me.
On trial like they tossed a suit at me.

Homophobic soldiers pierced eyes
like I'm only birth thighs
from a distance
met with resistance.
Mad because they couldn't nail me.
Hateful like if I crossed them.

I was in her praise
the way she'd gaze.
I was blessed.

Told too many times
that I need to confess.
Asked too many questions
about the way I was dressed
clothes too baggy for my breast.

Left to be shamed but I arose again.
She was my rose and friend.
Told them a man can penetrate me
yet only a woman
can penetrate my heart.

She was my guilty pleasure.
Devouring her like the forbidden fruit.
Many believe what we do to be tasteless.
Had priest look at me faceless.
Didn't lose my faith just said, 3 Hail Marys
and let's face this.

I closed my eyes, let him hold me
yet his chilling breath
could not compare to her warm wind.
God gave us will
but I couldn't love him if I tried.

Was a lie
to embrace his strong arm and sweat
to let him prod me like meat
serve him as King
when my Queendom was full of love
when my Heaven was in her arms.

**You can call me a sinner
but her kiss is forgiveness.**

Sustenance

Does love taste different?
When she is ripened
is she more fragrant with fidelity?

When you peel past her skin
is her soul sustenance, savory
her ambitions admirable, ambrosia?

Is she fruitful with fascination?

Does she yield seeds for you?

Larger Love

When I was free to embrace the world
the way I once loved her
I swear the flowers inclined
to smell the sweetness on my skin
scent solace.

The sun woke to my light.
The man on the moon awakened the dreaming
howling at my boundless sky.

Fall Away

Fall away like a feather off a wing
like a petal from a rose
like a samara off a maple tree.

Fall away like a silent tear
like a hand letting go
like the hair I once brushed
from your cheek.

Slowly, gracefully
if you must go.

Nourish Cruz was born and raised in New Jersey. She identifies as a Latina and is a proud member of the LBGTQ+ community. She began her journey into poetry at the age of 11 then started a successful transition into Spoken Word and Poetry Slam Competitions at the age of 15. Nourish is a board member and volunteer at A.C.P Arts, a non-profit that promotes diversity and awareness of social challenges by artistic expression. When she's not working her day job in the medical field, you can find her devouring cupcakes, hiking, binge-watching Angelina Jolie movies and writing her poetry.

Made in the USA
Monee, IL
29 May 2021